Foreseeing the Journey

POEMS BY JAMES APPLEWHITE

Foreseeing the Journey

LOUISIANA STATE UNIVERSITY PRESS

BATON ROUGE AND LONDON   1983

Publication of this book has been supported by a grant from the National Endowment
for the Arts in Washington, D.C., a federal agency.

The following poems originally appeared in these publications: "Crossing Over,"
Hampden-Sydney Poetry Review; "The Terminal," "The Ravine," "White Lake," "Notes
from a Journal by the River," *Southern Poetry Review;* "First by the Sea," "The Visitor,"
Carolina Quarterly; "Rheumatic Fever," "The Lumber Mill Fire," *Chowder Review;* "A Cap-
sized Boat," "Iron Age Flying," *Poets in the South;* "A Broken Lake," "Red Wing Hawk,"
Poetry Miscellany; "The Station," *Texas Review;* "Blood Ties: For Jan," *Mississippi Review;*
"Grandfather Noah," *St. Andrews Review;* "The Scene," "Beyond the Romantic Destina-
tion," *Virginia Quarterly Review;* "Science Fiction," *Poetry;* "View from a Tower," *The
Lyricist;* "Blackberries," *Mudfish;* "*Southland* Drive-In," "Trying to Drive Away from the
Past," "Passing the Marquee in Maysville," *Green River Review;* "That Which Is," *New
Jersey Poetry Journal;* "Foreseeing the Journey," *American Poetry Review;* "Canoe Trip: The
Last Afternoon," "Morning Prayer: To the Son," "Returning from the River," *Interna-
tional Poetry Review.*

LIBRARY OF CONGRESS CATALOGING IN PUBLICATION DATA

Applewhite, James.
  Foreseeing the journey.

  I. Title.
PS3551.P67F66 1983   811'.54   82-17165
ISBN 0-8071-1079-5
ISBN 0-8071-1080-9 (pbk.)

For my parents
James William Applewhite
Jane Elizabeth Mercer Applewhite
with all love

CONTENTS

Foreseeing the Journey

CROSSING OVER
(Somerset, by the Bristol Channel)

We hung suspended in the liquid of our time:
Sunshine of day after day as it streamed in our eyes.
Like riverbass about to spawn, we waited for a signal,
A sand grain going downstream, with all our world in it,
Or cloud-edge conjunction between a branch, the sun, and a bird.
Wind lifted leaves, blown hair was flash-bulbed on retinas.
Like photographs in boxes, these glimpses kept safe, with sewing
And models, behind an attic's one window. A garden fed children
In the seasons: with tomatoes, squash on quick stems.
Our youngest outgrew the older boy's clothes,
That house with garden lost behind mileage of vans.
One trip was closed in gilt leather, untouched by movers,
Waiting by a brass lamp base, in a lighted circle.

Even in that room closed to wind, the glitter would blur
In our South's sunlight, surnames, places, floating
Clear on a glaze from china and jewelry—outings,
Dinners, like a tumble of pressed flowers, photographs.
We had planned to rise clear of the dazzle, go ahead
Five hours across a dark Atlantic.

*   But with glass casing*
Signet and charter, we heard only echoes
In passages, under cathedrals and museums.
No pinnacled clock by river or tower of execution
Seemed the body of an all-wise past we had plotted to enter.
No Constable or Turner made London an Aladdin's cave.
Drawn by Coleridge's story, we ended at Porlock.

Now sun on the Bristol Channel builds a house of rays
Which frightens me. The pendulum moon sways
This parent of rivers, and current runs backward,
Seethes in pebbles like our aggregated moments.
The consciousness of Newton sun-swung this earth within
Space and force; I shrink within lines of his theorems.
Landscapes and weathers take our hearts. A house whose clocks
Are the sun and the moon draws geometries too large for emotion,

Though windows in its walls may possess us: sea-cliff and the panes
Of haze as shadow walks rocks, sky-colored budleigh,
Cut fields of straw, with hedgerows quilting far yellow.

On this beach like the valley of a poet-Cain, strange
As the moon, the fist-sized stones have turned back my wife.
I am left to the company of headlands, which shoulder into mist
Like great ships' recession, hulls of a navy out to sea.
Time's museum stands as great as any two lives are small.
I hold to green days with each other, innocent of other lands.

Our former selves still walk on the other Atlantic shore.
Their destination shows, clearer than if glimpsed from the plane.
Arthur's Tintagel was for them like a diagram in shadow,
Original stone behind tapestries of meadows and streams.
A castle exists, as huge as any country, with cornerstones
In soil and in the mind. Sometimes that land is England.

Iron Age Flying

Damn these charters. Past midnight
Already. I'm tired and hungry.
There's Miller from Iowa, getting her burger.
She asked me to dinner in London.
A generalization, every woman I've ever known.
Why am I flying alone? We've lived
So terribly closely. There has to be distance.

But leaving by myself feels somehow like dying.
It all keeps going before my eyes.
The garden I dreamed was the hub
Of the world, a place in the mind,
Where Alice waits behind the looking-glass.
We went beside the barn when we wanted:
Crack fat white, little pout smile.
Grandfather's windows looked over the tree. . .
Who told thee that thou wast naked?

The time going on, the time standing still:
Bookcase glass held reflections,
Smears on the air across titles in gilt.
And ghostlier wisps,
Breaths of us children
A day in winter when the stove went out.
Air was an hourglass
We breathed inside: sand grain memories.
Time seems running back again.
When we spun to get dizzy on the fish pond grass,
Lilies had momentum of their own,
Bushes encircling the pole of our eyes:
Centered before time.

I'd better get a bite before we board.
The dream kept returning,
A man in green on horseback.
Bricks in the wall seemed compacted of the dust
From old sun. Sky grew thick,

Like light summer evenings, with things spinning in it.
Horizontal lightning struck through the smoke,
And men fell off horses under trees.

Ah, a table with the *New York Times*.
I'm weary of this history of war,
Wilderness crossings in fear.
Let the sand slide back to its center,
To the land of a child's words again.

The beach was in sand grains with skins from the foam.
When I looked up squinting, sun in my lashes
Was broken colored glass, like windows in a church.
A wave between the sand pile hills when I turned
Looked as slick as rubber or a whale's hind flipper.
I thought him grass-shaggy in a hill rising up,
With waterfalls stabbing into the sun's fire circle,
But when God made a flood in the Bible for Noah,
People built cities, and wouldn't stay holy,
And other animals swam underneath the water.

Wet was in air and
In wind all around me.
Breathing was like our pond.
Lilies went with gold fish
In the mirror.
What I felt in my eyes and skin
Was part of what I was,
So then I was big.
The angel nurses
Stuck me with needles.
It made me feel as little
As a bird or a squirrel.

They let me come home,
To hollyhocks ruffled by a window,
Where a hummingbird's wings
Were as waving as cellophane.
His ice pick bill
Went in flowers like dresses.

If my ankles ached I wasn't thirsty.
They let me lie on the side porch couch,
But light was still dingy like the screens.
When father came early he would mow our lawn.
The blades whirled fast like a hummingbird's wings.
Under the pecan tree in air getting grayer,
Lightning bugs winked yellow, then gone. Pockets
In his overalls bulged big as muscles with money.
The way he was walking, leaning to the mower,
So it hummed grass bits into air's shining atoms,
Was becoming a memory. The shape of his strength
Would save me from fever, by mowing forever.
The tree stretched to keep itself in light,
Lightning bugs in it in clouds, as when
Sparks keep rising if you stir up a bonfire.

THE VISITOR

It had felt like being adopted,
When I first came home from the tower of rooms,
Where clouds looked in at the windows.
Always afterwards,
A point stayed sharp in my stomach,
Like love or being afraid,
To make where I was look strange,
But to understand the other peoples' lives,
That I glimpsed under shades
In upstairs windows going by in a car,
So the gypsy girls with curly oily hair
At carnivals in fall
Would seem familiar as sisters.

We were floating out already from the bank.
Vines tangled thick,
Like the moths' snow drifting around his sign,
So I thought of his station at the other end of town
With bulbs burning soon,
But here straight down was the color of dirt
And yet a shining mirror. I had to bend low
While his rope lashed back,
As if from whipping it to start.

Leaves beside my eyes went in rain-streaming lines,
And the creek looked as shiny as a hall,
If the floor is just waxed.
I leaned toward the light when a log
Underwater reared us over in slow motion,
With our boat in the center,
As if inside the spinning-by pond and fence,
When we'd whirl to get dizzy on the grass,
And browncold wet where the sky ought to be—
The not-breathing dark seemed sleeping awake
Till mosquitoes sang light in vines on the bank.

He saved me the same way his Esso sign
Would keep away darkness,
With moths all around it,
The station's roof raised up on columns
To balance the creek and night at the other end of town:
Saved me so his square of bright bulbs
Was floating on a water under sleep.

I had watched these trees get gradually bigger,
Coming at me crookedly like veins in old hands.
When I climbed down roots in their straggling shadow,
It made me shiver, like going in swimming.
Leaves between walls smelled of wet by my face,
Where an overhung ledge was dripping on ferns
So they nodded like puppets. On blue clay close
To the water, I would see the sand bar with raccoons'
Footprints, and notice in the bank where current had cut it
These shells of mussels, and oysters, and scallops,
Too deep in roots for somebody to have buried.
In a wet clay shadow like a long time ago,
I realized the ocean must have hidden them there.
I had read about dinosaurs' times, when the water
Had been higher, and had heard it in a shell up to my ear.
But I didn't just stay in the damp, I cut out
A scallop shell perfect and secret, closed up
With mud inside it, then climbed back up,
To see our town's plan simple in the distance,
Houses laid out like a child's wooden blocks,
And Christmas lights burning on our water tank already.
The ravine had reminded me of our boat turning over,
But now I had come back into light on my own.
Air tasted good when I breathed the cold sun.

As we drove from the dark, his shape looked flat
Against red, like a toy soldier made of cardboard.
He was cooling off his gas pumps with a hose. Tanks
Across the street reflected fire, silver-round
Flickering bombs, as the water squirted on.
A fireman yelled out about a tanker parked there,
Where it might explode. Father started running,
And mother caught me back from behind, and was screaming
His name. Smoke swirled so thick he disappeared.
The men said *look out*, but the wind blew then,
And I saw him in the cab, bent over toward the motor.
The truck jerked once and then stalled, while fire
Licked all around the back, then finally it rolled.
He drove across the road, into Wainwright's yard,
When a lid blew off with a firecracker explosion,
To go sailing high in the air, before it fell
Like the blade of a harrow making sparks on the road.
Father dived out but it didn't blow up;
I wanted us to help till it was out, but mother
Said we'd wait across the creek, so father drove
Us all past the stoplight, then in between stores,
And underneath trees high as clouds, till we had passed
Both churches and our house, when I thought about Moses
With his red sea behind, because gasoline would wash
In an ocean of burning, if the tanks burst she said,
So he drove the dark hill until the bridge went by,
And animals prowled like unfrightening nightmares.

I was walking on the ball field one evening, and light
Getting gray. Suddenly things didn't seem real.
The infield sand still warm to our toes,
And our clothes that were smelling like weeds, from
Running in the outfield, seemed distant and strange.
Being there with Teaky and Babs, us children,
Seemed as wonderful as anything in fairy tales.
I had to have lived it all already, and had
Forgotten to pretend that I was little a minute,
And was looking at three children from in the air.
Then was entering into who I was again, surprised:
Smell of weeds in my eyes, the diamond in shadow.

The sawmill's whistle for noon would surprise us,
When it sounded so loud and close by. Afterward,
The noises felt farther away, and we thought
About living in the country by ourselves.
Our map to the camp looked serious and older.
The creek lined a border at the bottom,
Dark limbs marking the thickets. Then fields
With regular, combed-looking furrows held
New corn sparkling like broken green bottles
In rows in the sun. Backyards fenced off
From the plowed-up dirt kept chickens and gardens,
Then the town's white houses followed streets,
And railroad tracks were ridged like a backbone.
The side toward the creek went down into night,
But coming toward the stoplight seemed up into sun.
Our station burned bulbs above its columns,
And the sawmill cut lumber out of trees,
So carpenters could nail up new houses, and people
Move in, and look through the upstairs windows
Into air from the lonesome edge of town—
The map in my mind now brighter in consciousness.

A BROKEN LAKE

We had on our bathing suits already in the car.
The plush seats prickled our bare legs, while the fields
Stayed level, with just the water-looking heat
In a waver over rows toward woods at the back
Like the dark behind a mirror.
Tobacco with broad leaves as in drawings with Indians,
And clouds white-flat in the horizon, looked strange
And shimmering, like the painted scenery in movies,
When the cowboy is riding by himself a long time
And the mountains stay the same.
Then all of a sudden we could see the right house,
With a china ball tree and a tire for a swing,
And uncle was turning onto nothing but a path,
Just two dirt tracks with weeds down the middle.
To our right, willows with their leaves like little fish
Showed where the water stayed hidden.
It seemed a green eye, with bushes for its lashes.
We wanted to be the first to go in, but the spell
Of that stillness was like a skin across our tunnel.
It was standing and running, or holding breath and breathing:
Waiting on the dirt hot as pavement, where beyond,
The water looked smooth and alive, with circles
Spreading out from where a dragonfly had touched,
A mirror for the clouds, that would break if we entered.

Finally we ran through the bushes, and splashed up
Clear spray, and went under with the feeling of breathing.
But one time a black snake as long as a man
Was twisting through the trees that made a gate.
Alice stood frozen, her eyes looking dazed.
The sand pit afterward felt strange in my mind,
As if a crack was invisibly in the light.
The snake's black mark through the air left a scar.

His boat in our lake, bull in a pasture,
Was towing this innertube he'd got from a tractor
And the doctor's wife in her two-piece suit
Like girls wore in movies was floating inside,
Laughing and turning in that rubber doughnut
That bobbled and stretched so a wave washed on it,
And pushed her suit top loose before she knew,
So I saw her breasts bright in the sun. We picnicked
Like nothing had happened, except that, remembering
Her breasts, the blood felt uneasy in my eyes.
Her face made me blink and look down like a light.

Now when I drove to the sand pit, the horizon
Through currents of mirage would gleam like an illusion,
A curtain which might open. The red wing hawk
Seemed especially for me, his appearance a sign.
I walked across furrows, which crumbled into ashes
In the heat, and prayed to see a hawk:
Swimming and flying in the liquid air,
Metallic as museums' bronze statues in the sun.
And one was there spiraling, tiny as a leaf
In a whirlpool, spinning as we used to on the grass.
He slanted with wings fixed open and motionless
And passed over me speechless in the dust, my arms raised
High and fingers spread wide for his wing tips,
While his face looked as fierce as Egyptian carvings:
A glinting from inside me expressed in the sky—
As if yellow eyes in sunlight were answering prayer.

I saw us from the hawk's point of view,
Saw us shrink in our quilted fields,
The houses, growing small enough for models, taken in
By a glance, with doll-figured people here and there,
And directions extending with memories and seasons,
Alice to the east among hyacinths
Where the light was new born,
Our station to the north with catalogues for motor parts,
The creek to the south where an odor of water
Went down a long way, our school field
To the west that was always autumn
With trees turning scarlet from absorbing sunsets.
I thought about father in a fragrance of grass,
Mowing in the quick-falling dark,
Or in his speedboat dangerously on the floods,
With all mortal heroes.

I felt now I wanted to be a great inventor,
Or heroic discoverer. Winters, experimenting outside,
I boiled rank chemicals over a pyramid of sticks,
Or heated crushed coal in a can on the hearth,
Until smoke through the tube was a gas I ignited.
I watched father welding, soot-smeared as Vulcan,
Masked,in black hood with rectangular eye-piece.
Wanting to invent my own system, I generated
Oxygen and hydrogen, mixed them in a jug.
The chem lab was silent when I forced out a jet
With incoming water, that lit hissing cutting
Into metal, till it exploded like a grenade.
I kept on with chemistry, saturated solutions
In beakers, grew crystals with parallel facets,
Watched through a microscope as water fleas gave birth.

Mechanix Illustrated and *Popular Science*
Were my favorite readings, as I fantasized a knowledge
Explaining the mystery my life seemed lost in.
But auto garages held mechanics bowed
Under hoods—in the religion of cylinder and piston.

Our Esso station faced its mirror-image station,
Where red-haired Rooster sold the beer father hated.
As wings gathered soft around our bulbs, blacks
From the vague dirt streets passed live through our light:
Glad-colored as moths or long-feathered birds.
Their shirts' blood-crimsons, gold or green blouses,
Sang within my eye like birdcall. They gathered
In flocks to Rooster's, buying Budweiser and Miller's,
Blue Ribbon and Schlitz. Stragglers
Now and then fell to us for Pepsis,
Or a brown boy exactly my height wanted money
Of pleasure, the gold foil condoms I dispensed
From the high shelf box with an envious knowledge.
Sundays, seated among our Puritan colors,
I remembered the blouses like tropical birds;
A sympathy perched with clipped wings within me,
Or fluttered with the scarlet-shirted
Bloods crossing out of our lights,
Into creekwater Saturday dark across fields,
Pockets enriched by the gold coins I sold.

In the forty-nine Ford I had earned,
We printed our tires
Into dirt below our special tree.
Ascending on wings
Of insects and leaves, we flew
In a slippage that was tight
And all freedom
On a wind above
Corn in the dark.

Our blood in an updraft column
Lifted off
In a suspended moment
Out of touch with the earth
As if endless
Like a fountain evanescent under lights
Till it burst
Toward the stars
Like our bonfire sparks at night

And then drifting
Winking out
Until lightning bugs hovering
In a honeysuckle odor
When we raised our heads to the window again
Were scattered over fields
Like embers of burning
As if we'd seeded the air with our fire.

Our bodies retreated,
Blood flowing west toward the long-gone sun.
We lay back happy
But hushed, mute and grave,
Afraid of the permanence of the love we had made,
Afraid of our knowledge: two after Eden.

Rimmed in by cypresses, tin water flashed
Like the top of a can, in fields still buzzing
With cicadas: electrical August short-circuiting.
The surface slicked over us like oil, shone
Silver with clouds. We walked, holding hands,
Toward the rides. Roller Coaster. Dive Bomber.
We sat in the Ferris Wheel, throbbing
With its engine, as it hurried us backward,
To show a black polish, the lake like marble
Under stars, bulbs on its opposite shore
Rolling across reflection in miniature pearls.

With a wince of thrill in the quick of our spines,
We offered up ourselves to a turning as enormous
As the seasons or desire, whirled down to search
Shadows, where water lapped subtly at roots,
For a place we could lie down together, wandered
Through glare from the lighted piers.
In the rides park afterward, there were dolls
To be won by rings or thrown balls. Pandas,
Like drunken guests at a wedding, faced
A tree-tall whirling as if spun by a giant.

I visited my cousin on the Pamlico, remembering
Our crabbing in the marsh grass shallows as children:
Our pine board cottage under shadow of the river,
Its color. Brown needles, brown water odor.
There had been talk then of Mr. Brougham,
As we heard tugs reverberate upstream,
Melancholy, metallic, echoing the word
Sanitorium. Brougham, Brougham, with wind
Through pines whistling thin as a cough—
Like scratchings of a broom against tombstones.

Now we revisited the Washington waterfront,
Toured old barges, demasted schooners,
Decks and bridges as in the Sargasso Sea;
Felt soil leach from the roots, trees
Topple over with houses in their grip,
Faces and rooms, many as in cities—
A city of ships—entering that current.

I encountered you freshman year—
You strange bird from the mountains,
Me half-unconscious from the coastal plain.
I made you my generous tempter,
Worldly-wise purveyor of the Bird's sad jazz,
Of records where Billie sang the absinthe-flavor
We had tasted only in Baudelaire.
Such times. The best and the worst. As when,
Half-bombed from Mayola's, you yelled
"Eat shit" at two Lambda Chi's,
One of them a slab-sided middleweight wrestler,
Who punched my face on the parking lot cinders
Until I kicked him and staggered away.

Literature went straight against the grain
Of that place. Pinnacles and spires held
The slumber of Oxford. Mechanical engineers
Occupied the quad, slide rules in holsters.
But Blackburn stood erect in our thoughts, a giant,
Live body asserting its right to be whole
Against the horizon's encroaching abstractions:
Men as of metal in that post-war world,
Professors as generals, grants for decorations.

Mentor and buddy, you *believed* in Rimbaud.
Orpheus as Narcissus, you tore yourself
In pieces on the mirror of the river.
Poetry, if poetry were possible, must be
A self-distillation by suffering, suicide
Of consciousness down *des Fleuves impassibles.*
The Bird's high notes in "Star Eyes"
Glimmered on oil near rats' shadow wharves.

I played learning's Hamlet, plotting dumb shows
Against a king I detested: whether general, physician,
Or literary scientist, who practiced his analysis
By quantitative measure: bibliography by the inch.
Blackburn's paranoia was greater than my own.
His figure stood erect in my thoughts, a giant,
Live body asserting its right to be whole
Against the horizon's encircling specters: cyclops
Skeletons with Martian death ray, stalking us
From *War of the Worlds*, great metal bodies
And a brain with tentacles, intellect uprooted,
Monstrous, divided in abstraction, unfeeling.

The Army Air Force in World War Two:
B-17's against Schweinfurt, Regensburg, in daylight.
Head full of war, I walked toward work:
Attendant on the psychiatric ward.

I wore a white coat on Meyer, kept keys,
Wheeled our prisoners toward the preparation for shock.
Dr. Lowenbach was Father, with his own apparatus
For the current, to knock them unconscious first jolt.
"De patient vants to be punished, so ve *punish.*"
A therapist in rubber gloves at the head
Held electrodes in each hand, placed one
On either temple. Their poor flesh clenched
Like a fist while he handled the switch, their jaws
Splintering paddles. Doctor Frankenstein
Administered their coming back to life.
Some showed burns, their eyes stared vacantly.
Ashby was the sporting alcoholic,
Was red-hued from liquor and sunburn on fairways.
With hand out he leaped, reached for my key,
Toppled us both. I held him on the floor.
I listened to the building's breathing, panted
Myself. Ashby conversed with the vent,
Cursed Doctors Pickerel, Lowenbach, and staff.
"No, no, not here," Mr. Ashby insisted,
"But God, come for me. The building's on fire."
I heard pained cries in the forced air's rumbling,
Heard the persistent voices of children, old men,
Women, being consumed by flames, fire storms
Twisting steel skeletons of cities.

The cemetery slope, grass after frost,
Looked pale as their hair. Earth's swells rolled,
An ocean of uncertain footing. My townspeople
Walked it to pay last respects, Nell Overman's
Round hat against the horizon, above her drawn-back
Shoulders, Norwood Whitley rubbing his blue jaw,
Planting steps heavily as if in boots to the knee,
Ann Louise Stanton moving soberly in her frock,
These Christians fallible across wintry grass
Which called them down, there to face the dying
Of W. H. Applewhite, gold name on a window,
Though the general store was his own no longer;
Who'd lived with the sun, the returns of plowing,
His devotion inscribed in two rows of his garden.
I imagined his figure, bowed to the handplow,
Old man half-kneeling within the order of seasons.

The people still moved in a stream, as I had seen
Them down steps of our church, Wainwright's round head,
His one crippled shoulder turning that hand inward,
My community as individually weathered as the trees,
Coming from inside, where I had sat in their power,
While flowers opened upward with notes of the organ.
The bronze coffin, magnified by the intense
Eyes of that full congregation, seemed massive,
Oblong, as I had imagined King Arthur's barge.

Borne up the aisle on townsmen's shoulders,
It seemed the vessel of hereditary identity,
Profoundly measured, onto seas past knowing.
I watched through the window as earth fell in waves,
The bronze box burning in my thoughts, an ark
Of my covenant, ark of this succeeding Noah,
King whom I would ride with on water till doomsday.

I
What's the red light? Oh Boarding Boarding.
I'm walking down a ramp into a tunnel.
Jesus, it's raining. Top of the plane
Seems a wet slick whale's back.
Jonah to England, with my sins
All upon me.
Why does it feel so like dying?
Riding the river in the speedboat with father,
I didn't feel fearful.
I wasn't so personal.
A kid's just anyone,
One drop of light into the sun's bright water.

Inside it's a cave.
Maybe find a seat by a window.
Important personalities are Cadillacs.
Black shams, limousines
Appropriate for funerals. The child soul inside.
How do you believe in this idiotic century?
I wasn't inventing the things I remembered.
Father as if mowing the evening,
Light as if in particles of dust—
But they were shining.
Seatbelt. Good, we're moving.

Faster and faster. Like rising
Toward heaven. Is this how it will be?
Regret and desire. Memories.
The red fire jumping as if speaking in tongues.
He drove away the tanker for our lives, through
The gasoline sea of her fear.
                    *
My neck feels cramped. What time
Could it be? Must have been asleep.
Move the pillow from the window.
And *where* could we be?

With lights down below.
A city. A galaxy.
Beautiful with distance and darkness.
Perhaps my life,
If seen from that remove—
With irregular beads, it becomes a necklace
Stringing a peninsula—
Are there rocks by the lights and black-foil water?
It's a bay within the land's last arms.

II
We are going and we have been.
To climb along the Somerset headlands:
Like hulks without sail
Resurrected from an underground England.

We'll scramble clay holes through
Iron age forts—no stones of Camelot—
Considering the blades from Saxon barrows.

Iron age, hand
In a rusty glove, handle
My throat, my thoughts,
Gently.

I began with a boy, whose sight
Was marked by a snake.
Though his brown time drains
With the Pamlico River,
Everything seen in his life
Flows in an underground stream
Where a new sun burns.

Over our horizon to the east, in constant
Night of the earth's own shadow
Which cones standing still
So that children, animals, weeds and jewels

Spin through it, a vision
Lies buried
Like treasure, one gleaming
Bearing the world revolves on:
Earth-lidded eyeball, wink of the cyclops.

Underground sun, give us prospect
On our landscape's mud, our poor map of paths
Which spins, recombines, in the head,
Spooling in thread
Red with the dye of real sheepfolds,
To stitch incorrigible imagination's pastoral.

Iron age flying, over
Planet's body where the dawn still hides,
Telescope fields, contours
Planted and a garden not realized.
Egg of earth holds the sun inside.

Foreseeing the Journey

I wrestle the American Actual:
Legs, oysters. Huge signboards
From close up at night. I went
To the dump, as if to weigh and count
Those flies like pebbles, black as crows;
Unloaded the refuse of our past,
Waved goodbye to a brassiere
As the spiked wheels passed over.
Unable to sleep, at the truck
Stop at two I found the waitress
Still alive, while trash was pounded
Deeper into the ground, Juggernaut
Dozer tottering on a flood of belongings,
Boxes leaking nylons and letters:
Cardboard movie in the head, catsup
Or blood. I wrestle the wheel
With the man on the dump as his caterpillar
Wallows like a skiff in breakers
On the flood of this undammed spillage.

I'll stand under billboards at night,
Their lights ten feet off the ground,
Wish myself a giant in the posters
For truckers. I wave three-dimensionally
To eyes charting warily toward Kansas City.

This is the obligatory Southern poem.
Will copperheads horny with venom twine
Cornerstones of mansions left charred by Sherman?
Listen, the field is paved, the only crop
Raised these speakers on poles. They crackle
With rumor, to boys with hand on the stick-shift,
Of the virgin who died impaled, after
Coca-Cola laced with Spanish Fly.
Fried chicken is eaten, not all the meat
Here is white, but even as a thunderhead
Slashes and cannonades, rendering heat
Into current, this living theater of bodies
Plays out its music—like a radio tuned
To a station from so far away, maybe
Latin America, its reception sounds eerie
With static and distance. Antennas catch
Signals from ditches, where frogs no bigger
Than the gonad-shaped pecans of the grove
Blow their bellies up to broadcast: *no matter,*
They say from the water, *we all here is*
Dark meat. Blacks run away to the swamps,
Slick with the rapes you wish your sisters.
The root of this plot, upraised on the screen,
Is poor white meat. And a wind comes
Sighing from the crowd, the great thundercrowd
In the mind of this Southern land. Some rain
Has fallen, little rivers trickled on the banks
Of back seats. Moccasins slide a soft water.

In the powerline cut
Seem to have sprung up like fencing,
A native barbed wire. Berries shine
As black-slick as beetles, yet
Sweet, sweet with a quinine aftertaste.
The seeds' tough purpose grinds in my teeth.
My skin almost lovingly
Clings to these thorns, stretched
In little pinnacles: as if pinned
To a frame. The clay which suits their nature
Must be old sun baked to brick light.
Earth red as Mars, as scarred,
You hold me like the body of a barbarous lover.

The monsters of the brain are
Filmed against stars.
Sometimes they appear
Long-fingeredly slender
As a tree able to walk
In pure dream. Jellies on stalks
Bear others, ovarian eyes
Awake in a blue light. Space's
Embryo claws to our faces.
They come from the titanium future,
Bringing computer as character.
Yet the bright castles in vacuum
Reveal a subterranean
Rooting: Gothic underland
With coffin. Frankenstein's hand
Stitches circuits, cleverer
With copper than once with cadaver.

Ills bequeathed as to children
Infect robot and alien.
Still, we voyage toward Eden.
Blue planet, Earth-like, hidden
In coordinates, how beautiful you are,
Dangled against backgrounds of stars.
Eyeball seeing no evil,
We prick you against our will.

Storefronts cardboard in streetlight
And shadow, moviehouse midway the stoplights.
Shirley Temple wore her lily dresses
On screen. Linda Blair, Brooke Shields,
Kristy McNichol, publicly unbosom
In whorehouse scripts, consigned to the devil.
What quality of face in the stripling,
Like Huckleberry Finn with tits,
Crossing into night where the red light held,
Exploitable water of innocence
Already dry behind those eyes?
What do we extract from their precocious screams—
Some slick bright thing like sap from a stem?
I remember as a child in an overgrown
Yard, absently striking the lilies
In a luxury of violation.

Something may be happening to the heart.
I repeople the highway, sidewalk, denuded
As by a flashbulb sun
With trees choiring one beyond the other.
Why do I conjure up holocaust?
I see it is a trick of this busy aether, a buzzing
About this tower as of its wasps.

My death is unreal. I climb
From the perspective of wires, confess blank
Ignorance, sense of sleight-of-hand
And an impudent fakery in our accustomed world, the news:
Reportages coming true like bad detective novels.

I play at their conceptions, but the luminous box,
Its tiny people, is less vivid
Than our cardboard Christmas armory with soldiers.
My time is like the spectrum of a star:
The bands then were wider and colored,
Summerlawn came back again next year.
Birthday sherbet oranged crystal
Against the high reflecting air, holding
Silver for the Thanksgiving seasons in its permanent cabinet.
A calendar wheel went forward, but touched
The same ground, which was green.
Now the sequence is fast-spun film,
It is gray and the intervals diminish.

Prosaic wailing with your woe
From everywhere, diminishing our capacity to be moved,
Allow us silence in which to love as we can;
Release to us time in its wholeness,
Relinquish the linear progress, these powerline
Towers like seven league crutches
That step across the ever-farther hills:
Perspective that narrows into a Future.

Yet earth still swings in its orbit, sun
Plays the alchemist to base vacancy.
Seeds as if down-shafted from the stars
Raise antennae to the seasonal telemetry, bear
Spring encoded in nodules of twig ends. Only
Our reason resists these signals: burgeoning, locality.

Is it the raw edge
Of air, season's unraveling,
Oak limbs frayed
To loose threads in the distance—
Or inconsequence
Of faces and acquaintance,
Desire jarred loose
As from disconnected wires?
Powerlines follow into
The country, a habit,
Transformers bulky shoulders
On poles. A child's question:
What is real?
And the traffic
Simonized to suave sexuality,
Bobcat, Cougar,
Chromium animals mounting
Onto the wind.
Rusted and dented. Old buckets.

I see, as through grains
Of coal dust in bins,
Through flyspecked screens
Of old summer, willow
Oaks leaning,
Narrow leaves spinning,
Boring into my seeing,
Each an awl.
How is it connected?
I crouch on the kerosene tank
Painted red on the darkening
Back porch. The kid's
Big brothers circle
Menacingly on their bikes.
I opened his cheek with a rock.
Fictions of the news,
The underground silos,

Stories I might have imagined,
Still disbelieve.
How can it be said
We live as we conceive?
I am unable to put
The sequence together:
Still the boy for whom
Rock was inspiration—
Like coming awake in this world.

Wastes of my life reflect from these clay flats
   With fennel as from plate glass windows:
Barber shops—emporia for pimples, white wall
   Haircuts, jokes about new uses for the tongue.
Today, where branches seem wrought Spanish railings,
   The cliff-face woodland opens in. I see
Countries more essential than any I've suspected,
   With well-ordered forest slopes and deer.
Such fantasies follow from the pewter, copper green,
   The antique leather, of a few last leaves—
Though the new lands imagined are haunted by the past.
   Though the fields here are peopled with faces,
Misery and poverty I can never do anything about.
   Basketball goals in projects hang rim-bent,
With white threads of nets, like a thousand-time
   Shredded virginity: the boys who played so often
Still one-on-one, eyeball to eyeball.
   Their score is still nothing to nothing.

She was holding
The pole through her pony
Carefully, as if the joy
Might dry, the brass
Shaft of its musical
Rise and fall turn dull.

Her father stood watching
In surplus fatigue. Black, slight,
He gave me, with his eye,
Permission to share in her victory
There over shyness and capturing
Delight on the wood horse fearfully.

A woman had picked up a dollar
With lips of her crotch in the silver
Dollar trailer. A sweat of humanity
Sizzled with onions, the lights' whirl
Musical and profane. I carried carefully
A girl's holding a brass pole.

December   Seeing the blue heron, I decided
Not to write a "dead animal poem":
Its eye gelatinous agate, color like
Ice that has crusted from a puddle,
A slate not hoveringly "high" anymore,
The sad electrocution too apparent—
Skin burned from shin—under powerlines
Crossing the river.

January   Later, the eye
A dead crater, everything else quite
Still in the cold, beak so homely,
A pot-handle substance, I was confirmed.

February   Now with it all mysteriously gone,
I waver. What was its color?
That slate-blue horizon through the trees?
Its shape was a wader of borders.
Its neck crooks back, a question-mark absence.
Its body was literal and common
That first frozen day: the stream
Iced hard, unmoving. But each day's sun,
With quickening heron in flight,
Now pulses through the faces of the leaves,
Of my child my wife.

Why has the landscape always to be leading,
Spelling with wind-sibilancies a suspended meaning,
Insinuating with wire-tangled-twigs the thorn
Of an archaic script, bark like old iron
Gating a road that goes to the horizon,
A tree the Lost City's column?
Do women share this search for destination?
Or is it errant but knightly man, aligning
Each pine wood into arcades, projecting
His nave into the wild limbs' vaulting,
Pursuing the body he explores unto exhaustion?
Afterward, what is there to promise or hide
For either woman or countryside?
Isn't there only the pushing-through of saplings and briars,
The ordinary effort of stepping from rock to rock?
No river courses all of waterfall or cataract.
What of later, at leisure, no act
But simple stare into water, as still years
Suspend into pools? Better
One place then than many another, a weather
Holding cabin and a tree: so clear as to obscure
The valleys always farther but never farther understood.
One stream seethes with seas beyond the wood.

The fan inhales one continuous breath: through
This upstairs room I am lying awake in, foreseeing the journey.
This creek, this street, this one row of houses, diagram Town.
As simple as the world. As air and the light. Old birthplace.
Tomorrow we'll go with the current, canoe around snags—
As I guide my son through the thicket of childhood—
Past moccasins uglier than the Biblical serpent.
Passion-flowers as in Rousseau's jungles.

This four-bladed beating, as of great hawks crossed,
Sucks moths from their flight, with light's
Exhalation, draws foil-glint wings from the corn.
Its rumble surrounds me. Our bungalow lifts off, zeppelin
With roof, shadow more angled than a biplane bomber.
I seem Huck Finn visiting a house on the flood.
Books from around me hover their pages. With Zane Grey
And Edgar Rice Burroughs, presents bobbing up like helium
In the attic—my Christmas models in a loose formation—
I fly in the flock of these presences, owls with the heads
Of dead relatives, the photograph of my mother's brothers
Sailing in the ghost wind, until the huge cry they feel
Becomes one with the wailing of the fan,
This rest what I can do and no more fear.

Almon who told me the Cyclops' blinding
Looks so beautiful there, delicate of feature, shy
With sister, ignorant of the years of high school teaching,
The loneliness to come. But not consumed
By my mother's weeping, for all who have died,
Her father Mercer's fall under his buggy,
I fly in this house and its history
As in Lord Greystoke's plane above the trees.
Would any of us be born into the world
If we had it to do over?
Through this sleep of the unborn and of spirits
The propeller tom-toms a message.

The attic fan in this window, ill-designed,
Dangerous, great blades unshielded, drive belt
Exposed to the unwary night walker,
Put in by my father in jack-leg fashion
Like everything down east, by him who lost
His fingers to an air compressor belt,
Seems the risk of all living. I'm flying too high
But in the dawn light chill I reach down
To find a blanket green as leaves.
I pull up the jungle over my body.

Vines in the ironwoods, the poplars
And cypresses, grape vine in black oak,
Boles broken-armed in the river
Rotting silver, willows and birches
Suavely clustered, as clouds' soles
Trail bodies blue as flesh: my son
On the sandpoint is fishing, current is flashing—
And I breathe a surprise from this wind,
That swamp ooze dripping from undercut banks,
The cups of fossil shells running over,
Could simplify and purify
To this bright salt sense this
Scrubbed absolute of weather on the river—
Where field drainings, aerated,
Mix no scent of the physical pastures with
Premonition of ocean.

Our boat is drifting. And filling.
My brother or son in the bow
Can't breathe green shadows
Of algae. For his sake I strike
With the paddle, cross a sky
With black pearl, magnetic
Mirror with peaks in its depths:
Dragon-mountain. Or woman.
I pole onto sand. A tentacle
Stings from memory: swimming
With snakes, her dark flesh roots.
Falling through the lens of this pond,
I swim a negative's reversal.
I pray as the son steps ashore,
As sun wheels his head with bright spokes:

May I wrestle the sheets and awake,
From each thing becoming its opposite,
As fire enters water like mating.
May I arise from metamorphosis
Where quick eels couple with waterfall
Lightning, the eye opens to burrow
Itself in mud, blind with creation.
Hold me, as once you held Proteus,
Till I have taken my one shape.

A Man's life of any worth is a continual allegory. . . . Keats

Setting out Eastward, I follow
   The river, a slant illumination
Like summer's fire there below

Each footstep. The path I run
   Twists between hardwoods and pines,
As if into aperture of the sun.

Streaming of breath intertwines
   With twigs, a moment's wind
Caged like birds within vines.

What seems the river's far bend
   Proves a stream whose bank
Ends this path, where I stand

And consider, before turning back.
   Resigned to returning as I went,
I hope blue heron or deer track

Will solace this sense of midpoint
   Passed, as shadow of my body
At its feet, layering the present

Onto the past, is re-running history.
   Where a sycamore opens womb-hollow,
I'm scratched by briars of puberty.

My sight into Future is shadow.
   Ghost winds polish the river
But bend no grass as they blow.

Marriage is textured by cedar
    With hollies. One yellow hickory,
Like Goldilocks' hair in November

By three-bear pines, seems a nursery
    I remember, a tale which I tell
This further time. Now I foresee

Where the root threatens ankle,
    In sun without glare, come clear
From behind, on a trail grown double.

Continuing is returning, each year
    I visit closer to my death
And to my birth. A briar

Catches shoelace, the path
    Dead-ends into the rotten log
Of scholarship, though moss underneath

Lets the child's hand stroke his dog:
    Prologue to struggles, committees,
Poison ivy thicket and bog.

Our path through schoolyard trees
    Followed hill which went
Home at night. My knees

Like an old man's now, back bent,
    I climb to its long plateau,
Where oaks remembered and present

Form the one landscape I know.
My infant heart in a body
Imitating age, I see glow

From a window through knowledge's Tree.
Thanatos' branches bar light
Of Eros' luminous body.

That kerosene lamp seems to beat,
A dark sun pulsing heat:
Lets me finish at the start.